Contents

INTERNATIONAL CONVENTION FOR SAFE CONTAINERS, 1972

CSC

2014 EDITION

Su'

IMO
INTERNATIONAL MARITIME ORGANIZATION
London, 2014

First published in 1983
by the INTERNATIONAL MARITIME ORGANIZATION
4 Albert Embankment, London SE1 7SR
www.imo.org

Sixth edition 2014

Printed by Polestar Wheatons (UK) Ltd, Exeter, EX2 8RP

ISBN: 978-92-801-1593-2

IMO PUBLICATION
Sales number: IC282E

This publication has been prepared from official documents of IMO, and every effort has been made to eliminate errors and reproduce the original text(s) faithfully. Readers should be aware that, in case of inconsistency, the official IMO text will prevail.

075396

Foreword

The rapid increase since the 1950s in the use of freight containers for the consignment of goods by sea and the development of specialized container ships, prompted the International Maritime Organization (IMO), in 1967, to study the safety of containerization in marine transport.

In 1972, a conference jointly convened by the United Nations and IMO was held to consider a draft convention prepared by IMO in cooperation with the Economic Commission for Europe.

The 1972 Convention for Safe Containers (CSC 1972) adopted by that conference has two goals: one is to maintain a high level of safety of human life in the transport and handling of containers by providing generally acceptable test procedures and related strength requirements which have proven adequate over the years; the other is to facilitate the international transport of containers by providing uniform international safety regulations, equally applicable to all modes of surface transport. In this way, proliferation of divergent national safety regulations can be avoided.

The requirements of CSC 1972 apply to the great majority of freight containers used internationally, except those designed specifically for carriage by air. As it was not intended that all container, van or reusable packing boxes should be affected, the scope of the Convention is limited to containers of a prescribed minimum size having corner fittings.

CSC 1972 sets out procedures whereby containers used in international transport must be approved for safety by the Administration of a Contracting Party or by an organization acting on its behalf. The Administration, or an organization authorized by it, will then authorize the manufacturer to affix a Safety Approval Plate containing the relevant technical data onto approved containers.

The approval evidenced by the Safety Approval Plate granted by one Contracting Party should be recognized by other Contracting Parties. This principle of reciprocal acceptance of approved containers constitutes the cornerstone of the Convention. Once approved and plated, containers are expected to move in international transport with the minimum of safety control formalities. The subsequent maintenance of a container approved for safety is the responsibility of the owner, who is required to have the container periodically examined.

The technical annexes to CSC 1972 specifically require that the container should be subjected to various tests, which represent a combination of safety requirements of both the inland and maritime modes of transport. Flexibility is incorporated into the Convention by the provision of simplified amendment procedures for the technical annexes.

CSC 1972 was amended in 1981 to provide transitional arrangements for plating of existing containers (which had to be completed by 1 January 1985) and for the marking of the date of the container's next examination by 1 January 1987.

It was again amended in 1983 to extend the interval between re-examinations to 30 months and to permit a choice of container re-examination procedures between the original periodic examination scheme or a new approved continuous examination programme.

In 1991, amendments were adopted to annex I to prevent containers being marked with misleading maximum gross weight information, to ensure removal of the Safety Approval Plate when void for any reason and to provide for the approval of modified containers. Amendments to annex II clarified certain test provisions. The 1991 amendments entered into force on 1 January 1993.

In 1993, amendments to the Convention were adopted by resolution A.737(18) but have not yet entered into force.

Amendments to the Convention adopted by resolution MSC.310(88) entered into force on 1 January 2012 and include new specifications regarding Safety Approval Plates, describing the validity of, and elements to be included in, approved examination programmes; a new test for containers being approved for operation with one door removed; and the addition of a new annex III on control and verification. Annex III provides specific control measures for authorized officers to assess the integrity of structurally sensitive components of containers and to decide whether a container is safe to continue in transportation or whether it should be stopped until remedial action has been taken.

The amendments to the Convention adopted by resolution MSC.355(92) enter into force on 1 July 2014 and include new definitions at the beginning of annexes I and II, along with consequential amendments to ensure uniform usage of terminology throughout CSC 1972; amendments to align all physical dimensions and units to the SI system; the introduction of a transitional period for marking containers with restricted stacking capacity; and the inclusion in annex III of the list of deficiencies which do not require an immediate out-of-service decision by the control officer but do require additional safety measures to enable safe ongoing transport. These new amendments incorporate many elements of the 1993 amendments. However, as they are not identical to the 1993 amendments and to avoid any confusion, this publication does not include resolution A.737(18).

The supplement to this publication, containing revised and consolidated recommendations on harmonized interpretation and implementation of CSC 1972, and guidelines for development of an approved continuous examination programme, does not constitute any part of the Convention.

International Convention for Safe Containers, 1972

Preamble

THE CONTRACTING PARTIES,

RECOGNIZING the need to maintain a high level of safety of human life in the handling, stacking and transporting of containers,

MINDFUL of the need to facilitate international container transport,

RECOGNIZING, in this context, the advantages of formalizing common international safety requirements,

CONSIDERING that this end may best be achieved by the conclusion of a convention,

HAVE DECIDED to formalize structural requirements to ensure safety in the handling, stacking and transporting of containers in the course of normal operations, and to this end

HAVE AGREED as follows:

Article I
General obligation under the present Convention

The Contracting Parties undertake to give effect to the provisions of the present Convention and the annexes hereto, which shall constitute an integral part of the present Convention.

Article II
Definitions

For the purpose of the present Convention, unless expressly provided otherwise:

1 *Container* means an article of transport equipment:

(a) of a permanent character and accordingly strong enough to be suitable for repeated use;

(b) specially designed to facilitate the transport of goods, by one or more modes of transport, without intermediate reloading;

(c) designed to be secured and/or readily handled, having corner fittings for these purposes;

(d) of a size such that the area enclosed by the four outer bottom corners is either:

(i) at least 14 m^2 (150 sq ft) or

(ii) at least 7 m^2 (75 sq ft) if it is fitted with top corner fittings.

The term *container* includes neither vehicles nor packaging; however, containers when carried on chassis are included.

2 *Corner fittings* means an arrangement of apertures and faces at the top and/or bottom of a container for the purposes of handling, stacking and/or securing.

3 *Administration* means the Government of a Contracting Party under whose authority containers are approved.

4 *Approved* means approved by the Administration.

5 *Approval* means the decision by an Administration that a design type or a container is safe within the terms of the present Convention.

6 *International transport* means transport between points of departure and destination situated in the territory of two countries to at least one of which the present Convention applies. The present Convention shall also apply when part of a transport operation between two countries takes place in the territory of a country to which the present Convention applies.

7 *Cargo* means any goods, wares, merchandise and articles of every kind whatsoever carried in the containers.

8 *New container* means a container the construction of which was commenced on or after the date of entry into force of the present Convention.

9 *Existing container* means a container which is not a new container.

10 *Owner* means the owner as provided for under the national law of the Contracting Party or the lessee or bailee, if an agreement between the parties provides for the exercise of the owner's responsibility for maintenance and examination of the container by such lessee or bailee.

11 *Type of container* means the design type approved by the Administration.

12 *Type-series container* means any container manufactured in accordance with the approved design type.

13 *Prototype* means a container representative of those manufactured or to be manufactured in a design type series.

14 *Maximum operating gross weight* or *rating* or *R* means the maximum allowable combined weight of the container and its cargo.

15 *Tare weight* means the weight of the empty container including permanently affixed ancillary equipment.

16 *Maximum permissible payload* or *P* means the difference between maximum operating gross weight or rating and tare weight.

Article III

Application

1 The present Convention applies to new and existing containers used in international transport, excluding containers specially designed for air transport.

2 Every new container shall be approved in accordance with the provisions either for type-testing or for individual testing as contained in annex I.

3 Every existing container shall be approved in accordance with the relevant provisions for approval of existing containers set out in annex I within five years from the date of entry into force of the present Convention.

Article IV

Testing, inspection, approval and maintenance

1 For the enforcement of the provisions of annex I every Administration shall establish an effective procedure for the testing, inspection and approval of containers in accordance with the criteria established in the present Convention, provided, however, that an Administration may entrust such testing, inspection and approval to organizations duly authorized by it.

2 An Administration which entrusts such testing, inspection and approval to an organization shall inform the Secretary-General of the Inter-Governmental Maritime Consultative Organization (hereinafter referred to as "the Organization")* for communication to Contracting Parties.

* The name of the Organization was changed to "International Maritime Organization" by virtue of amendments to the Organization's Convention which entered into force on 22 May 1982.

3 Application for approval may be made to the Administration of any Contracting Party.

4 Every container shall be maintained in a safe condition in accordance with the provisions of annex I.

5 If an approved container does not in fact comply with the requirements of annexes I and II the Administration concerned shall take such steps as it deems necessary to bring the container into compliance with such requirements or to withdraw the approval.

Article V

Acceptance of approval

1 Approval under the authority of a Contracting Party, granted under the terms of the present Convention, shall be accepted by the other Contracting Parties for all purposes covered by the present Convention. It shall be regarded by the other Contracting Parties as having the same force as an approval issued by them.

2 A Contracting Party shall not impose any other structural safety requirements or tests on containers covered by the present Convention, provided, however, that nothing in the present Convention shall preclude the application of provisions of national regulations or legislation or of international agreements, prescribing additional structural safety requirements or tests for containers specially designed for the transport of dangerous goods, or for those features unique to containers carrying bulk liquids or for containers when carried by air. The term *dangerous goods* shall have that meaning assigned to it by international agreements.

Article VI

Control

1 Every container which has been approved under article III shall be subject to control in the territory of the Contracting Parties by officers duly authorized by such Contracting Parties. This control shall be limited to verifying that the container carries a valid Safety Approval Plate as required by the present Convention, unless there is significant evidence for believing that the condition of the container is such as to create an obvious risk to safety. In that case the officer carrying out the control shall only exercise it in so far as it may be necessary to ensure that the container is restored to a safe condition before it continues in service.

2 Where the container appears to have become unsafe as a result of a defect which may have existed when the container was approved, the Administration responsible for that approval shall be informed by the Contracting Party which detected the defect.

Article VII

Signature, ratification, acceptance, approval and accession

1 The present Convention shall be open for signature until 15 January 1973 at the Office of the United Nations at Geneva and subsequently from 1 February 1973 until 31 December 1973 inclusive at the Headquarters of the Organization at London by all States Members of the United Nations or Members of any of the specialized agencies or of the International Atomic Energy Agency or Parties to the Statute of the International Court of Justice, and by any other State invited by the General Assembly of the United Nations to become a Party to the present Convention.

2 The present Convention is subject to ratification, acceptance or approval by States which have signed it.

3 The present Convention shall remain open for accession by any State referred to in paragraph 1.

4 Instruments of ratification, acceptance, approval or accession shall be deposited with the Secretary-General of the Organization (hereinafter referred to as "the Secretary-General").

Article VIII

Entry into force

1 The present Convention shall enter into force twelve months from the date of the deposit of the tenth instrument of ratification, acceptance, approval or accession.

2 For each State ratifying, accepting, approving or acceding to the present Convention after the deposit of the tenth instrument of ratification, acceptance, approval or accession, the present Convention shall enter into force twelve months after the date of the deposit by such State of its instrument of ratification, acceptance, approval or accession.

3 Any State which becomes a Party to the present Convention after the entry into force of an amendment shall, failing an expression of a different intention by that State,

(a) be considered as a Party to the Convention as amended; and

(b) be considered as a Party to the unamended Convention in relation to any Party to the Convention not bound by the amendment.

Article IX

Procedure for amending any part or parts of the present Convention

1 The present Convention may be amended upon the proposal of a Contracting Party by any of the procedures specified in this article.

2 Amendment after consideration in the Organization:

(a) Upon the request of a Contracting Party, any amendment proposed by it to the present Convention shall be considered in the Organization. If adopted by a majority of two thirds of those present and voting in the Maritime Safety Committee of the Organization, to which all Contracting Parties shall have been invited to participate and vote, such amendment shall be communicated to all Members of the Organization and all Contracting Parties at least six months prior to its consideration by the Assembly of the Organization. Any Contracting Party which is not a Member of the Organization shall be entitled to participate and vote when the amendment is considered by the Assembly.

(b) If adopted by a two-thirds majority of those present and voting in the Assembly, and if such majority includes a two-thirds majority of the Contracting Parties present and voting, the amendment shall be communicated by the Secretary-General to all Contracting Parties for their acceptance.

(c) Such amendment shall come into force twelve months after the date on which it is accepted by two thirds of the Contracting Parties. The amendment shall come into force with respect to all Contracting Parties except those which, before it comes into force, make a declaration that they do not accept the amendment.

3 Amendment by a conference:

Upon the request of a Contracting Party, concurred in by at least one third of the Contracting Parties, a conference to which the States referred to in article VII shall be invited will be convened by the Secretary-General.

Article X

Special procedure for amending the annexes

1 Any amendment to the annexes proposed by a Contracting Party shall be considered in the Organization at the request of that Party.

2 If adopted by a two-thirds majority of those present and voting in the Maritime Safety Committee of the Organization to which all Contracting Parties shall have been invited to participate and to vote, and if such majority includes a two-thirds majority of the Contracting Parties present and voting, such amendment shall be communicated by the Secretary-General to all Contracting Parties for their acceptance.

3 Such an amendment shall enter into force on a date to be determined by the Maritime Safety Committee at the time of its adoption unless, by a prior date determined by the Maritime Safety Committee at the same time, one fifth or five of the Contracting Parties, whichever number is less, notify the Secretary-General of their objection to the amendment. Determination by the Maritime Safety Committee of the dates referred to in this paragraph shall be by a two-thirds majority of those present and voting, which majority shall include a two-thirds majority of the Contracting Parties present and voting.

4 On entry into force any amendment shall, for all Contracting Parties which have not objected to the amendment, replace and supersede any previous provision to which the amendment refers; an objection made by a Contracting Party shall not be binding on other Contracting Parties as to acceptance of containers to which the present Convention applies.

5 The Secretary-General shall inform all Contracting Parties and Members of the Organization of any request and communication under this article and the date on which any amendment enters into force.

6 Where a proposed amendment to the annexes has been considered but not adopted by the Maritime Safety Committee, any Contracting Party may request the convening of a conference to which the States referred to in article VII shall be invited. Upon receipt of notification of concurrence by at least one third of the other Contracting Parties, such a conference shall be convened by the Secretary-General to consider amendments to the annexes.

Article XI

Denunciation

1 Any Contracting Party may denounce the present Convention by effecting the deposit of an instrument with the Secretary-General. The denunciation shall take effect one year from the date of such deposit with the Secretary-General.

2 A Contracting Party which has communicated an objection to an amendment to the annexes may denounce the present Convention and such denunciation shall take effect on the date of entry into force of such an amendment.

Article XII
Termination

The present Convention shall cease to be in force if the number of Contracting Parties is less than five for any period of twelve consecutive months.

Article XIII
Settlement of disputes

1 Any dispute between two or more Contracting Parties concerning the interpretation or application of the present Convention which cannot be settled by negotiation or other means of settlement shall, at the request of one of them, be referred to an arbitration tribunal composed as follows: each party to the dispute shall appoint an arbitrator and these two arbitrators shall appoint a third arbitrator, who shall be Chairman. If, three months after receipt of a request, one of the parties has failed to appoint an arbitrator or if the arbitrators have failed to elect the Chairman, any of the parties may request the Secretary-General to appoint an arbitrator or the Chairman of the arbitration tribunal.

2 The decision of the arbitration tribunal established under the provisions of paragraph 1 shall be binding on the parties to the dispute.

3 The arbitration tribunal shall determine its own rules of procedure.

4 Decisions of the arbitration tribunal, both as to its procedures and its place of meeting and as to any controversy laid before it, shall be taken by majority vote.

5 Any controversy which may arise between the parties to the dispute as regards the interpretation and execution of the award may be submitted by any of the parties for judgement to the arbitration tribunal which made the award.

Article XIV
Reservations

1 Reservations to the present Convention shall be permitted, excepting those relating to the provisions of articles I to VI, XIII, the present article and the annexes, on condition that such reservations are communicated in writing and, if communicated before the deposit of the instrument of ratification, acceptance, approval or accession, are confirmed in that instrument. The Secretary-General shall communicate such reservations to all States referred to in article VII.

2 Any reservation made in accordance with paragraph 1:

(a) modifies for the Contracting Party which made the reservation the provisions of the present Convention to which the reservation relates to the extent of the reservation;

(b) modifies those provisions to the same extent for the other Contracting Parties in their relations with the Contracting Party which entered the reservation.

3 Any Contracting Party which has formulated a reservation under paragraph 1 may withdraw it at any time by notification to the Secretary-General.

Article XV
Notification

In addition to the notifications and communications provided for in articles IX, X and XIV, the Secretary-General shall notify all the States referred to in article VII of the following:

(a) signatures, ratifications, acceptances, approvals and accessions under article VII;

(b) the dates of entry into force of the present Convention in accordance with article VIII;

(c) the date of entry into force of amendments to the present Convention in accordance with articles IX and X;

(d) denunciations under article XI;

(e) the termination of the present Convention under article XII.

Article XVI
Authentic texts

The original of the present Convention, of which the Chinese, English, French, Russian and Spanish texts are equally authentic, shall be deposited with the Secretary-General, who shall communicate certified true copies to all States referred to in article VII.

IN WITNESS WHEREOF the undersigned Plenipotentiaries, being duly authorized thereto by their respective Governments, have signed the present Convention.*

DONE at Geneva this second day of December, one thousand nine hundred and seventy-two.

* Signatures omitted.

Annex I
Regulations for the testing, inspection, approval and maintenance of containers

Chapter I
Regulations common to all systems of approval

General provisions

The following definitions shall be applied for the purpose of this annex:

The letter *g* means the standard acceleration of gravity; *g* equals 9.8 m/s^2.

The word *load,* when used to describe a physical quantity to which units may be ascribed, signifies mass.

Maximum operating gross mass or *Rating* or *R* means the maximum allowable sum of the mass of the container and its cargo. The letter *R* is expressed in units of mass. Where the annexes are based on gravitational forces derived from this value, that force, which is an inertial force, is indicated as *Rg*.

Maximum permissible payload or *P* means the difference between maximum operating gross mass or rating and tare. The letter *P* is expressed in units of mass. Where the annexes are based on the gravitational forces derived from this value, that force, which is an inertial force, is indicated as *Pg*.

Tare means the mass of the empty container, including permanently affixed ancillary equipment.

Regulation 1
Safety Approval Plate

1 **(a)** A Safety Approval Plate conforming to the specifications set out in the appendix to this annex shall be permanently affixed to

every approved container at a readily visible place, adjacent to any other approval plate issued for official purposes, where it would not be easily damaged.

(b) On each container, all maximum operating gross mass markings shall be consistent with the maximum operating gross mass information on the Safety Approval Plate.

(c) The owner of the container shall remove the Safety Approval Plate on the container if:

(i) the container has been modified in a manner which would void the original approval and the information found on the Safety Approval Plate, or

(ii) the container is removed from service and is not being maintained in accordance with the Convention, or

(iii) the approval has been withdrawn by the Administration.

2 **(a)** The plate shall contain the following information in at least the English or French language:

CSC SAFETY APPROVAL

Country of approval and approval reference

Date (month and year) of manufacture

Manufacturer's identification number of the container or, in the case of existing containers for which that number is unknown, the number allotted by the Administration

Maximum operating gross mass (kg and lb)

Allowable stacking load for 1.8*g* (kg and lb)

Transverse racking test force (newtons).

(b) A blank space should be reserved on the plate for insertion of end-wall and/or side-wall strength values (factors) in accordance with paragraph 3 of this regulation and annex II, tests 6 and 7. A blank space should also be reserved on the plate for the first and subsequent maintenance examination dates (month and year) when used.

3 Where the Administration considers that a new container satisfies the requirements of the present Convention in respect of safety and if, for such container, the end-wall and/or side-wall strength values (factors) are designed to be greater or less than those stipulated in annex II, such values shall be indicated on the Safety Approval Plate. Where the stacking or racking values are less than 192,000 kg or 150 kN, respectively, the container shall be considered as having limited stacking or racking capacity and shall be conspicuously marked, as required under the relevant standards,* at or before their next scheduled examination or before any other date approved by the Administration, provided this is not later than 1 July 2015.

4 The presence of the Safety Approval Plate does not remove the necessity of displaying such labels or other information as may be required by other regulations which may be in force.

5 A container, the construction of which was completed prior to 1 July 2014, may retain the Safety Approval Plate as permitted by the Convention prior to that date as long as no structural modifications occur to that container.

Regulation 2

Maintenance and examination

1 The owner of the container shall be responsible for maintaining it in safe condition.

2 **(a)** The owner of an approved container shall examine the container or have it examined in accordance with the procedure either prescribed or approved by the Contracting Party concerned, at intervals appropriate to operating conditions.

(b) The date (month and year) before which a new container shall undergo its first examination shall be marked on the Safety Approval Plate.

(c) The date (month and year) before which the container shall be re-examined shall be clearly marked on the container on or as close as practicable to the Safety Approval Plate and in a manner acceptable to that Contracting Party which prescribed or approved the particular examination procedure involved.

(d) The interval from the date of manufacture to the date of the first examination shall not exceed five years. Subsequent examination of new containers and re-examination of existing containers shall be at intervals of not more than 30 months. All examinations shall determine whether the container has any defects which could place any person in danger.

* Refer to current standard ISO 6346, Freight containers – Coding, identification and marking.

3 **(a)** As an alternative to paragraph 2, the Contracting Party concerned may approve a continuous examination programme if satisfied, on evidence submitted by the owner, that such a programme provides a standard of safety not inferior to the one set out in paragraph 2 above.

(b) To indicate that the container is operated under an approved continuous examination programme, a mark showing the letters **ACEP** and the identification of the Contracting Party which has granted approval of the programme shall be displayed on the container on or as close as practicable to the Safety Approval Plate.

(c) All examinations performed under such a programme shall determine whether a container has any defects which could place any person in danger. They shall be performed in connection with a major repair, refurbishment, or on-hire/off-hire interchange and in no case less than once every 30 months.

4 As a minimum, approved programmes should be reviewed once every 10 years to ensure their continued viability. In order to ensure uniformity by all involved in the inspection of containers and their ongoing operational safety, the Contracting Party concerned shall ensure the following elements are covered in each prescribed periodic or approved continuous examination programme:

(a) methods, scope and criteria to be used during examinations;

(b) frequency of examinations;

(c) qualifications of personnel to carry out examinations;

(d) system of keeping records and documents that will capture:

- **(i)** the owner's unique serial number of the container;
- **(ii)** the date on which the examination was carried out;
- **(iii)** identification of the competent person who carried out the examination;
- **(iv)** the name and location of the organization where the examination was carried out;
- **(v)** the results of the examination; and
- **(vi)** in the case of a periodic examination scheme (PES), the next examination date (NED);

(e) a system for recording and updating the identification numbers of all containers covered by the appropriate examination scheme;

(f) methods and systems for maintenance criteria that addresses the design characteristics of the specific containers;

(g) provisions for maintaining leased containers if different than those used for owned containers; and

(h) conditions and procedures for adding containers into an already approved programme.

5 The Contracting Party shall carry out periodic audits of approved programmes to ensure compliance with the provisions approved by the Contracting Party. The Contracting Party shall withdraw any approval when the conditions of approval are no longer complied with.

6 For the purpose of this regulation, *the Contracting Party concerned* is the Contracting Party of the territory in which the owner is domiciled or has his head office. However, in the event that the owner is domiciled or has his head office in a country the government of which has not yet made arrangements for prescribing or approving an examination scheme and until such time as the arrangements have been made, the owner may use the procedure prescribed or approved by the Administration of a Contracting Party which is prepared to act as the Contracting Party concerned. The owner shall comply with the conditions for the use of such procedures set by the Administration in question.

7 Administrations shall make information on approved continuous examination programmes publicly available.

Chapter II
Regulations for approval of new containers by design type

Regulation 3
Approval of new containers

To qualify for approval for safety purposes under the present Convention all new containers shall comply with the requirements set out in annex II.

Regulation 4
Design type approval

In the case of containers for which an application for approval has been submitted, the Administration will examine designs and witness testing of a prototype container to ensure that the containers will conform with the requirements set out in annex II. When satisfied, the Administration shall notify the applicant in writing that the container meets the requirements of the present Convention and this notification shall entitle the manufacturer to affix the Safety Approval Plate to every container of the design type series.

Regulation 5
Provisions for approval by design type

1 Where the containers are to be manufactured by design type series, application made to an Administration for approval by design type shall be accompanied by drawings, a design specification of the type of container to be approved and such other data as may be required by the Administration.

2 The applicant shall state the identification symbols which will be assigned by the manufacturer to the type of container to which the application for approval relates.

3 The application shall also be accompanied by an assurance from the manufacturer that he will:

- **(a)** produce to the Administration such containers of the design type concerned as the Administration may wish to examine;

(b) advise the Administration of any change in the design or specification and await its approval before affixing the Safety Approval Plate to the container;

(c) affix the Safety Approval Plate to each container in the design type series and to no others;

(d) keep a record of containers manufactured to the approved design type. This record shall at least contain the manufacturer's identification numbers, dates of delivery and names and addresses of customers to whom the containers are delivered.

4 Approval may be granted by the Administration to containers manufactured as modifications of an approved design type if the Administration is satisfied that the modifications do not affect the validity of tests conducted in the course of design type approval.

5 The Administration shall not confer on a manufacturer authority to affix Safety Approval Plates on the basis of design type approval unless satisfied that the manufacturer has instituted internal production-control features to ensure that the containers produced will conform to the approved prototype.

Regulation 6

Examination during production

In order to ensure that containers of the same design type series are manufactured to the approved design, the Administration shall examine or test as many units as it considers necessary, at any stage during production of the design type series concerned.

Regulation 7

Notification of Administration

The manufacturer shall notify the Administration prior to commencement of production of each new series of containers to be manufactured in accordance with an approved design type.

Chapter III
Regulations for approval of new containers by individual approval

Regulation 8
Approval of individual containers

Approval of individual containers may be granted where the Administration, after examination and witnessing of tests, is satisfied that the container meets the requirements of the present Convention; the Administration, when so satisfied, shall notify the applicant in writing of approval and this notification shall entitle him to affix the Safety Approval Plate to such container.

Chapter IV

Regulations for approval of existing containers and new containers not approved at time of manufacture

Regulation 9

Approval of existing containers

1 If, within five years from the date of entry into force of the present Convention, the owner of an existing container presents the following information to an Administration:

(a) date and place of manufacture;

(b) manufacturer's identification number of the container if available;

(c) maximum operating gross mass capability;

(d) **(i)** evidence that a container of this type has been safely operated in maritime and/or inland transport for a period of at least two years, or

(ii) evidence to the satisfaction of the Administration that the container was manufactured to a design type which had been tested and found to comply with the technical conditions set out in annex II, with the exception of those technical conditions relating to the end-wall and side-wall strength tests, or

(iii) evidence that the container was constructed to standards which, in the opinion of the Administration, were equivalent to the technical conditions set out in annex II, with the exception of those technical conditions relating to the end-wall and side-wall strength tests;

(e) allowable stacking load for 1.8*g* (kg and lb); and

(f) such other data as required for the Safety Approval Plate;

then the Administration, after investigation, shall notify the owner in writing whether approval is granted; and if so, this notification shall entitle the owner to affix the Safety Approval Plate after an examination of the container concerned has been carried out in accordance with regulation 2. The examination of the container concerned and the affixing of the Safety Approval Plate shall be accomplished not later than 1 January 1985.

2 Existing containers which do not qualify for approval under paragraph 1 of this regulation may be presented for approval under the provisions of chapter II or chapter III of this annex. For such containers the requirements of annex II relating to end-wall and/or side-wall strength tests shall not apply. The Administration may, if it is satisfied that the containers in question have been in service, waive such of the requirements in respect of presentation of drawings and testing, other than the lifting and floor-strength tests, as it may deem appropriate.

Regulation 10

Approval of new containers not approved at time of manufacture

If, on or before 6 September 1982, the owner of a new container which was not approved at the time of manufacture presents the following information to an Administration:

- **(a)** date and place of manufacture;
- **(b)** manufacturer's identification number of the container, if available;
- **(c)** maximum operating gross mass capability;
- **(d)** evidence to the satisfaction of the Administration that the container was manufactured to a design type which has been tested and found to comply with the technical conditions set out in annex II;
- **(e)** allowable stacking load for 1.8*g* (kg and lb); and
- **(f)** such other data as required for the Safety Approval Plate;

the Administration, after investigation, may approve the container, notwithstanding the provisions of chapter II. Where approval is granted, such approval shall be notified to the owner in writing, and this notification shall entitle the owner to affix the Safety Approval Plate after an examination of the container concerned has been carried out in accordance with regulation 2. The examination of the container concerned and the affixing of the Safety Approval Plate shall be accomplished not later than 1 January 1985.

Chapter V
Regulations for approval of modified containers

Regulation 11
Approval of modified containers

The owner of an approved container that has been modified in a manner resulting in structural changes shall notify the Administration or an approved organization duly authorized by it of those changes. The Administration or authorized organization may require retesting of the modified container as appropriate prior to recertification.

Appendix

The Safety Approval Plate, conforming to the model reproduced below, shall take the form of a permanent, non-corrosive, fireproof rectangular plate measuring not less than 200 mm × 100 mm. The words **CSC SAFETY APPROVAL**, of a minimum letter height of 8 mm, and all other words and numbers of a minimum height of 5 mm shall be stamped into, embossed on or indicated on the surface of the plate in any other permanent and legible way.

CSC SAFETY APPROVAL

1 [GB-L/749/2/7/75]

2 DATE MANUFACTURED . . . .

3 IDENTIFICATION No. . . . .

4 MAXIMUM OPERATING GROSS MASS . . . . kg . . . . . lb

5 ALLOWABLE STACKING LOAD FOR 1.8*g* . . . . kg . . . . . . lb

6 TRANSVERSE RACKING TEST FORCE . . . . newtons

7 . . . .

8 . . . .

9 . . . .

≥ 100 mm

≥ 200 mm

1 Country of approval and approval reference as given in the example on line 1. (The country of approval should be indicated by means of the distinguishing sign used to indicate country of registration of motor vehicles in international road traffic.)

2 Date (month and year) of manufacture.

3 Manufacturer's identification number of the container or, in the case of existing containers for which that number is unknown, the number allotted by the Administration.

4 Maximum operating gross mass (kg and lb).

5 Allowable stacking load for 1.8g (kg and lb).

6 Transverse racking test force (newtons).

7 End-wall strength to be indicated on plate only if end-walls are designed to withstand a force of less or greater than 0.4 times the gravitational force by maximum permissible payload, i.e. 0.4Pg.

8 Side-wall strength to be indicated on plate only if the side-walls are designed to withstand a force of less or greater than 0.6 times the gravitational force by maximum permissible payload, i.e. 0.6Pg.

9 First maintenance examination date (month and year) for new containers and subsequent maintenance examination dates (month and year) if plate is used for this purpose.

10 One door off stacking strength to be indicated on plate only if the container is approved for one door off operation. The marking shall show: **ALLOWABLE STACKING LOAD ONE DOOR OFF FOR 1.8*g* (... kg ... lb)**. This marking shall be displayed immediately near the stacking test value (see line 5).

11 One door off racking strength to be indicated on plate only if the container is approved for one door off operation. The marking shall show: **TRANSVERSE RACKING TEST FORCE ONE DOOR OFF (... newtons)**. This marking shall be displayed immediately near the racking test value (see line 6).

Annex II
Structural safety requirements and tests

General provisions

The following definitions shall be applied for the purpose of this annex:

The letter *g* means the standard acceleration of gravity; *g* equals 9.8 m/s^2.

The word *load,* when used to describe a physical quantity to which units may be ascribed, signifies mass.

Maximum operating gross mass or *Rating* or *R* means the maximum allowable sum of the mass of the container and its cargo. The letter R is expressed in units of mass. Where the annexes are based on gravitational forces derived from this value, that force, which is an inertial force, is indicated as *Rg*.

Maximum permissible payload or *P* means the difference between maximum operating gross mass or rating and tare. The letter *P* is expressed in units of mass. Where the annexes are based on the gravitational forces derived from this value, that force, which is an inertial force, is indicated as *Pg*.

Tare means the mass of the empty container, including permanently affixed ancillary equipment.

Introduction

In setting the requirements of this annex, it is implicit that, in all phases of the operation of containers, the forces as a result of motion, location, stacking and gravitational effect of the loaded container and external forces will not exceed the design strength of the container. In particular, the following assumptions have been made:

(a) the container will so be restrained that it is not subjected to forces in excess of those for which it has been designed;

(b) the container will have its cargo stowed in accordance with the recommended practices of the trade so that the cargo does not impose upon the container forces in excess of those for which it has been designed.

Construction

1 A container made from any suitable material which satisfactorily performs the following tests without sustaining any permanent deformation or abnormality which would render it incapable of being used for its designed purpose shall be considered safe.

2 The dimensions, positioning and associated tolerances of corner fittings shall be checked having regard to the lifting and securing systems in which they will function.

Test loads and test procedures

Where appropriate to the design of the container, the following test loads and test procedures shall be applied to all kinds of containers under test:

1 Lifting

The container, having the prescribed internal loading, shall be lifted in such a way that no significant acceleration forces are applied. After lifting, the container shall be suspended or supported for five minutes and then lowered to the ground.

A Lifting from corner fittings

Test load and applied forces	Test procedures
Internal load A uniformly distributed load such that the sum of the mass of container and test load is equal to 2*R*. In the case of a tank container, when the test load of the internal load plus the tare is less than 2*R*, a supplementary load, distributed over the length of the tank, is to be added to the container. **Externally applied forces** Such as to lift the sum of a mass of 2*R* in the manner prescribed (under the heading Test procedures).	(i) *Lifting from top corner fittings* Containers greater than 3,000 mm (10 ft) (nominal) in length shall have lifting forces applied vertically at all four top corner fittings. Containers of 3,000 mm (10 ft) (nominal) in length or less shall have lifting forces applied at all four top corner fittings, in such a way that the angle between each lifting device and the vertical shall be 30°. (ii) *Lifting from bottom corner fittings* Containers shall have lifting forces applied in such a manner that the lifting devices bear on the bottom corner fittings only. The lifting forces shall be applied at angles to the horizontal of: • 30° for containers of length 12,000 mm (40 ft) (nominal) or greater, • 37° for containers of length 9,000 mm (30 ft) (nominal) and up to but not including 12,000 mm (40 ft) (nominal), • 45° for containers of length 6,000 mm (20 ft) (nominal) and up to but not including 9,000 mm (30 ft) (nominal), • 60° for containers of length less than 6,000 mm (20 ft) (nominal).

B Lifting by any other additional methods

Test load and applied forces	Test procedures
Internal load A uniformly distributed load such that the sum of the mass of container and test load is equal to 1.25*R*. **Externally applied forces** Such as to lift the sum of a mass of 1.25*R* in the manner prescribed (under the heading Test procedures).	(i) *Lifting from fork-lift pockets* The container shall be placed on bars which are in the same horizontal plane, one bar centred within each fork-lift pocket which is used for lifting the loaded container. The bars shall be of the same width as the forks intended to be used in the handling, and shall project into the fork pocket 75% of the length of the fork pocket.
Internal load A uniformly distributed load such that the sum of the mass of container and test load is equal to 1.25*R*. In the case of a tank container, when the test load of the internal load plus the tare is less than 1.25*R*, a supplementary load, distributed over the length of the tank, is to be applied to the container. **Externally applied forces** Such as to lift the sum of a mass of 1.25*R* in the manner prescribed (under the heading Test procedures).	(ii) *Lifting from grappler-arm positions* The container shall be placed on pads in the same horizontal plane, one under each grappler-arm position. These pads shall be of the same sizes as the lifting area of the grappler arms intended to be used.
	(iii) *Other methods* Where containers are designed to be lifted in the loaded condition by any method not mentioned in A or B(i) and (ii), they shall also be tested with the internal loading and externally applied forces representative of the acceleration conditions appropriate to that method.

2 Stacking

1 For conditions of international transport where the maximum vertical acceleration varies significantly from 1.8*g* and when the container is reliably and effectively limited to such conditions of transport, the stacking load may be varied by the appropriate ratio of acceleration.

2 On successful completion of this test the container may be rated for the allowable superimposed static stacking load, which should be indicated on the Safety Approval Plate against the heading: **ALLOWABLE STACKING LOAD FOR 1.8*g* (... kg ... lb).**

Test load and applied forces	Test procedures
Internal load A uniformly distributed load such that the sum of the mass of container and test load is equal to 1.8*R*. Tank containers may be tested in the tare condition.	The container, having the prescribed internal loading, shall be placed on four level pads which are in turn supported on a rigid horizontal surface, one under each bottom corner fitting or equivalent corner structure. The pads shall be centralized under the fittings and shall be of approximately the same plan dimensions as the fittings.
Externally applied forces Such as to subject each of the four top corner fittings to a vertical downward force equal to 0.25 × 1.8 × the gravitational force of the allowable superimposed static stacking load.	Each externally applied force shall be applied to each of the corner fittings through a corresponding test corner fitting or through a pad of the same plan dimensions. The test corner fitting or pad shall be offset with respect to the top corner fitting of the container by 25 mm (1 in) laterally and 38 mm (1½ in) longitudinally.

3 Concentrated loads

Test load and applied forces	Test procedures
(a) On roof	
Internal load None. **Externally applied forces** A concentrated gravitational force of 300 kg (660 lb) uniformly distributed over an area of 600 mm x 300 mm (24 in x 12 in).	The externally applied forces shall be applied vertically downwards to the outer surface of the weakest area of the roof of the container.
(b) On floor	
Internal load Two concentrated loads, each of 2,730 kg (6,000 lb) and each added to the container floor within a contact area of 142 cm^2 (22 sq in). **Externally applied forces** None.	The test should be made with the container resting on four level supports under its four bottom corners in such a manner that the base structure of the container is free to deflect. A testing device loaded to a mass of 5,460 kg (12,000 lb), that is 2,730 kg (6,000 lb) on each of two surfaces, having, when loaded, a total contact area of 284 cm^2 (44 sq in), that is 142 cm^2 (22 sq in) on each surface, the surface width being 180 mm (7 in) spaced 760 mm (30 in) apart, centre to centre, should be manoeuvred over the entire floor area of the container.

4 Transverse racking

Test load and applied forces	Test procedures
Internal load None. **Externally applied forces** Such as to rack the end structures of the container sideways. The forces shall be equal to those for which the container was designed.	The container in tare condition shall be placed on four level supports, one under each bottom corner, and shall be restrained against lateral and vertical movement by means of anchor devices so arranged that the lateral restraint is provided only at the bottom corners diagonally opposite to those at which the forces are applied. The externally applied forces shall be applied either separately or simultaneously to each of the top corner fittings on one side of the container in lines parallel both to the base and to the planes of the ends of the container. The forces shall be applied first towards and then away from the top corner fittings. In the case of containers in which each end is symmetrical about its own vertical centreline, one side only need be tested, but both sides of containers with asymmetric ends shall be tested.

5 Longitudinal restraint (static test)

When designing and constructing containers, it must be borne in mind that containers, when carried by inland modes of transport, may sustain accelerations of $2g$ applied horizontally in a longitudinal direction.

Test load and applied forces	Test procedures
Internal load A uniformly distributed load such that the sum of the mass of a container and test load is equal to the maximum operating gross mass or rating, R. In the case of a tank container, when the mass of the internal load plus the tare is less than the maximum gross mass or rating, R, a supplementary load is to be added to the container. **Externally applied forces** Such as to subject each side of the container to longitudinal compressive and tensile forces of magnitude Rg, that is, a combined force of $2Rg$ on the base of the container as a whole.	The container, having the prescribed internal loading, shall be restrained longitudinally by securing the two bottom corner fittings or equivalent corner structures at one end to suitable anchor points. The externally applied forces shall be applied first towards and then away from the anchor points. Each side of the container shall be tested.

6 End-walls

The end-walls should be capable of withstanding a force of not less than 0.4 times the force equal to gravitational force by maximum permissible payload. If, however, the end-walls are designed to withstand a force of less or greater than 0.4 times the gravitational force by maximum permissible payload, such a strength factor shall be indicated on the Safety Approval Plate in accordance with annex I, regulation 1.

Test load and applied forces	Test procedures
Internal load Such as to subject the inside of an end-wall to a uniformly distributed force of $0.4Pg$ or such other force for which the container may be designed. **Externally applied forces** None.	The prescribed internal loading shall be applied as follows: Both ends of a container shall be tested except that where the ends are identical only one end need be tested. The end-walls of containers which do not have open sides or side doors may be tested separately or simultaneously. The end-walls of containers which do have open sides or side doors should be tested separately. When the ends are tested separately the reactions to the forces applied to the end-wall shall be confined to the base structure of the container.

7 Side-walls

The side-walls should be capable of withstanding a force of not less than 0.6 times the force equal to gravitational force by maximum permissible payload. If, however, the side-walls are designed to withstand a force of less or greater than 0.6 times the gravitational force by maximum permissible payload, such a strength factor shall be indicated on the Safety Approval Plate in accordance with annex I, regulation 1.

Test load and applied forces	Test procedures
Internal load Such as to subject the inside of a side-wall to a uniformly distributed force of $0.6Pg$ or such other force for which the container may be designed. **Externally applied forces** None.	The prescribed internal loading shall be applied as follows: Both sides of a container shall be tested except that where the sides are identical only one side need be tested. Side-walls shall be tested separately and the reactions to the internal loading shall be confined to the corner fittings or equivalent corner structures. Open-topped containers shall be tested in the condition in which they are designed to be operated, for example, with removable top members in position.

8 One door off operation

1 Containers with one door removed have a significant reduction in their ability to withstand racking forces and, potentially, a reduction in stacking strength. The removal of a door on a container in operation is considered a modification of the container. Containers must be approved for one door off operation. Such approval shall be based on test results as set forth below.

2 On successful completion of the stacking test, the container may be rated for the allowable superimposed stacking load, which shall be indicated on the Safety Approval Plate immediately below line 5: **ALLOWABLE STACKING LOAD FOR 1.8*g* ONE DOOR OFF (... kg and ... lb).**

3 On successful completion of the racking test, the transverse racking test force shall be indicated on the Safety Approval Plate immediately below line 6: **TRANSVERSE RACKING TEST FORCE ONE DOOR OFF (... newtons).**

Test load and applied forces	Test procedures
(a) Stacking	
Internal load A uniformly distributed load such that the sum of the mass of container and test load is equal to 1.8*R*.	The test procedures shall be as set forth under **2 STACKING.**
Externally applied forces Such as to subject each of the four top corner fittings to a vertical downward force equal to 0.25 × 1.8 × the gravitational force of the allowable superimposed static stacking load.	
(b) Transverse racking	
Internal load None.	The test procedures shall be as set forth under **4 TRANSVERSE RACKING.**
Externally applied forces Such as to rack the end structures of the container sideways. The forces shall be equal to those for which the container was designed.	

Annex III
Control and verification

1 Introduction

Article VI of the Convention refers to the control measures that may be taken by Contracting Parties. Such control should be limited to verifying that the container carries a valid Safety Approval Plate, and an approved continuous examination programme (ACEP) or a valid next examination date (NED) marking, unless there is significant evidence for believing that the condition of the container is such as to create an obvious risk to safety. This annex provides specifics to enable authorized officers to assess the integrity of structurally sensitive components of containers and to help them decide whether a container is safe to continue in transportation or whether it should be stopped until remedial action has been taken. The criteria given are to be used to make immediate out-of-service determinations, and should not be used as repair or in-service criteria under a CSC ACEP or a periodic examination scheme.

2 Control measures

Authorized officers should consider the following:

- **.1** control should be exercised on those containers that create an obvious risk to safety;
- **.2** loaded containers with damages equal to, or in excess of, the criteria set forth below are deemed to place a person in danger. The authorized officer should stop those containers. However, the authorized officer may permit the onward movement of the container, if it is to be moved to its ultimate destination without lifting from its current means of transport;
- **.3** empty containers with damages equal to, or in excess of, the criteria set forth below are also deemed to place a person in danger. Empty containers are typically repositioned for repair at an owner-selected depot provided they can be safely moved; this can involve either a domestic or an international move. Any damaged container being repositioned should be handled and transported with due regard to its structural deficiency;

.4 authorized officers should notify the container owner, lessee or bailee, as appropriate, whenever a container is placed under control;

.5 the provisions set forth in this annex are not exhaustive for all types of containers or all possible deficiencies or combination of deficiencies;

.6 damage to a container may appear serious without creating an obvious risk to safety. Some damage such as holes may infringe customs requirements but may not be structurally significant; and

.7 major damage may be the result of significant impact which could be caused by improper handling of the container or other containers, or significant movement of the cargo within the container. Therefore, special attention should be given to signs of recent impact damage.

3 Training of authorized officers

The Contracting Party exercising control should ensure that authorized officers tasked to carry out these assessments and control measures receive the necessary training. This training should involve both theoretical and practical instruction.

4 Structurally sensitive components

4.1 The following components are structurally sensitive and should be examined for serious deficiencies in accordance with the following table:

(i)	(ii)	(iii)	(iv)	(v)	(vi)	(vii)
Structurally sensitive component	**Serious deficiency requiring immediate out-of-service determination**	**Deficiency requiring advice to owner and restrictions for transport**	**Restrictions to be applied in case of deficiencies according to column (iii)**			
			Empty container		**Loaded container**	
			Sea transport	**Other modes**	**Sea transport**	**Other modes**
Top rail	Local deformation to the rail in excess of 60 mm or separation or cracks or tears in the rail material in excess of 45 mm in length (see note 1)	Local deformation to the rail in excess of 40 mm or separation or cracks or tears in the rail material in excess of 10 mm in length (see note 1)	No restrictions	No restrictions	Bottom lifting not allowed; top lifting allowed only by use of spreaders without chains	Bottom lifting not allowed; top lifting allowed only by use of spreaders without chains
	Note 1: On some designs of tank containers the top rail is not a structurally significant component.					
Bottom rail	Local deformation perpendicular to the rail in excess of 100 mm or separation or cracks or tears in the rail material in excess of 75 mm in length (see note 2)	Local deformation perpendicular to the rail in excess of 60 mm or separation or cracks or tears in the rail material: in excess of 25 mm in length in the upper flange; or of web in any length (see note 2)	No restrictions	No restrictions	Lifting at (any) corner fitting not allowed	Lifting at (any) corner fitting not allowed
	Note 2: The rail material does not include the rail's bottom flange.					

(i)	(ii)	(iii)	(iv)	(v)	(vi)	(vii)
Header	Local deformation to the header in excess of 80 mm or cracks or tears in excess of 80 mm in length	Local deformation to the header in excess of 50 mm or cracks or tears in excess of 10 mm in length	Container shall not be overstowed	No restrictions	Container shall not be overstowed	No restrictions
Sill	Local deformation to the sill in excess of 100 mm or cracks or tears in excess of 100 mm in length.	Local deformation to the sill in excess of 60 mm or cracks or tears in excess of 10 mm in length	Container shall not be overstowed	No restrictions	Container shall not be overstowed	No restrictions
Corner posts	Local deformation to the post in excess of 50 mm or cracks or tears in excess of 50 mm in length	Local deformation to the post in excess of 30 mm or cracks or tears of any length	Container shall not be overstowed	No restrictions	Container shall not be overstowed	No restrictions

(i)	(ii)	(iii)	(iv)	(v)	(vi)	(vii)
Corner and intermediate fittings	Missing corner fittings, any through cracks or tears in the fitting, any deformation of the fitting that precludes full engagement of the securing or lifting fittings (see note 3) or any weld separation of adjoining components in excess of 50 mm in length	Weld separation of adjoining components of 50 mm or less	Container shall not be lifted on board a ship if the damaged fittings prevent safe lifting or securing	Container shall be lifted and handled with special care	Container shall not be loaded on board a ship	Container shall be lifted and handled with special care
		Any reduction in the thickness of the plate containing the top aperture that makes it less than 25 mm thick	Container shall be lifted and handled with special care Container shall not be overstowed when twistlocks have to be used	Container shall be lifted and handled with special care	Container shall not be lifted by the top corner fittings	Container shall be lifted and handled with special care
		Any reduction in the thickness of the plate containing the top aperture that makes it less than 26 mm thick	Container shall not be overstowed when fully automatic twistlocks are to be used	Container shall be lifted and handled with special care	Container shall not be used with fully automatic twistlocks	Container shall be lifted and handled with special care
	Note 3: The full engagement of securing or lifting fittings is precluded if there is any deformation of the fitting beyond 5 mm from its original plane, any aperture width greater than 66 mm, any aperture length greater than 127 mm or any reduction in thickness of the plate containing the top aperture that makes it less than 23 mm thick.					

(i)	(ii)	(iii)	(iv)	(v)	(vi)	(vii)
Under-structure	Two or more adjacent cross members missing or detached from the bottom rails; 20% or more of the total number of cross members missing or detached (see note 4)	One or two cross members missing or detached (see note 4)	No restrictions	No restrictions	No restrictions	No restrictions
		More than two cross members missing or detached (see notes 4 and 5)	No restrictions	No restrictions	Maximum payload shall be restricted to 0.5*P*	Maximum payload shall be restricted to 0.5*P*
	Note 4: If onward transport is permitted, it is essential that detached cross members are precluded from falling free. **Note 5:** Careful cargo discharge is required as forklift capability of the understructure might be limited.					
Locking rods	One or more inner locking rods are non-functional (see note 6)	One or more outer locking rods are non-functional (see note 6)	Container shall not be overstowed	No restrictions	Container shall not be overstowed; cargo shall be secured against the container frame and the door shall not be used to absorb acceleration forces; otherwise maximum payload shall be restricted to 0.5*P*	Cargo shall be secured against the container frame and the door shall not be used to absorb acceleration forces; otherwise maximum payload shall be restricted to 0.5*P*
	Note 6: Some containers are designed and approved (and so recorded on the Safety Approval Plate) to operate with one door open or removed.					

4.2 The effect of two or more incidents of damage in the same structurally sensitive component, even though each is less than in the above table, could be equal to, or greater than, the effect of the single damage noted in the table. In such circumstances, the authorized officer may stop the container and seek further guidance from the Contracting Party.

4.3 For tank containers, the attachment of the shell to the container frame should also be examined for any readily visible serious structural deficiency comparable to that specified in the table. If any such serious structural deficiency is found in any of these attachments, the control officer should stop the container.

4.4 For platform containers with folding end frames, the end frame locking mechanism and the hinge pins about which the end frame rotates are structurally sensitive and should also be inspected for damage.

Supplement

CSC.1/Circ.138/Rev.1

Revised recommendations on harmonized interpretation and implementation of the International Convention for Safe Containers, 1972, as amended*

1 General

The various points concerning harmonized interpretation and implementation of the International Convention for Safe Containers, 1972 (CSC 1972), as amended, on which consensus has so far been reached are given below.

2 Definitions (article II, paragraphs 8 to 10)

2.1 *New container* and *existing container*. Where necessary, individual Administrations should determine the date on which the construction of a container shall be deemed to have commenced for purposes of determining whether a container should be considered as "new" or as "existing".

2.2 *Owner*, for the purpose of these revised recommendations, also includes the owner's local representative.

2.3 For the purposes of these revised recommendations, the following definitions are used:

- **.1** *depot* means a repair or storage facility or location; and
- **.2** *structurally sensitive components* means those container components that are significant in allowing the container to be safely used in transportation. They are listed under paragraph 10.4 below and shown in figures 1 to 5.

---

* The Maritime Safety Committee, at its ninety-second session (12 to 21 June 2013), approved the Revised recommendations on harmonized interpretation and implementation of the International Convention for Safe Containers, 1972, as amended (5 August 2013).

3 **Application** (article III, paragraph 1)

3.1 Swap bodies/demountables

3.1.1 It is agreed that CSC 1972 does not have to be applied to containers known as swap bodies/demountables and designed and used for carriage by road only or by rail and road only and which are without stacking capability and top lift facilities.

3.1.2 It is also agreed that CSC 1972 does not have to be applied to such swap bodies/demountables transported by sea on condition that they are mounted on a road vehicle or rail wagon. However, CSC 1972 does apply to swap bodies/demountables used in transoceanic services.

3.2 Offshore containers

It is agreed that CSC 1972 does not necessarily apply to offshore containers that are handled in open seas. Offshore containers are subject to different design, handling and testing parameters as determined by the Administration. Nonetheless offshore containers may be approved under the provisions of CSC 1972 provided the containers meet all applicable provisions and requirements of the Convention.*

3.3 Ship's gear carriers and bins

3.3.1 It is agreed that CSC 1972 does not necessarily apply to ship's gear carriers and bins, as skeletal platform-based containers with fixed end posts and associated storage bins used for the storage of twist-locks, lashing bars, etc., are not used for international transport as defined by this Convention and so are not containers as defined. However, these specialist containers are carried aboard container and other ships and are handled in the same way as all other containers, and therefore present the same risks during loading and discharging from the ship.

3.3.2 Consequently, it is recommended that these units should be included in a maintenance and examination scheme and subject to periodic inspections.

4 **Entry into force** (articles III and VIII)

All containers should be inspected and affixed with Safety Approval Plates by the Administration of the Contracting Party not less than five years from the date of entry into force of the Convention for that Party.

* Refer to Guidelines for the approval of offshore containers handled in open seas (MSC/Circ.860).

5 Testing, inspection and approval (article IV, paragraphs 1 and 2): selection of organizations entrusted to carry out these functions

Administrations will require a basic description of the organizations to be entrusted with testing, inspection and approval functions, together with evidence of their technical capability to carry this out, and will have to satisfy themselves as to the financial well-being of such organizations. The Administrations will, furthermore, have to satisfy themselves that the organizations are free from undue influence by any container owner, operator, manufacturer, lessor, repairer or other concerned party who may have a vested interest in obtaining container approval.

6 Approval of containers for foreign owners or manufacturers (article IV, paragraph 3) and reciprocity

6.1 Where possible, Contracting Parties should make every effort to provide facilities or means to grant approvals to foreign container owners or manufacturers seeking their approval of containers in accordance with the provisions of the Convention.

6.2 Approval of containers would be facilitated if classification societies or other organizations approved by one Contracting Party could be authorized to act for other Contracting Parties under arrangements acceptable to the parties involved.

7 Maintenance and structural modifications (article IV)

7.1 Development of detailed guidelines on standards of maintenance will create an unnecessary burden for Administrations attempting to implement the Convention as well as for owners. However, in order to ensure uniformity in the inspection of containers and their ongoing operational safety, the Contracting Party concerned should ensure the following elements are covered in each prescribed periodic or approved continuous examination programme:

.1 methods, scope and criteria to be used during examinations;

.2 frequency of examinations;

.3 qualifications of personnel to carry out examinations;

.4 system of keeping records and documents (see section 12 below);

.5 a system for recording and updating the identification numbers for all containers covered by the appropriate examination scheme;

.6 methods and systems for maintenance criteria that addresses the design characteristics of the specific containers;

.7 provisions for maintaining leased containers if different than those used for owned containers; and

.8 conditions and procedures for adding containers into an already approved programme.

7.2 All prescribed periodic or approved continuous examination programmes should be subject to a period of validity of the approval and shall be reviewed by the Administration not later than 10 years after approval or reapproval to ensure their continued viability.

7.3 Administrations should periodically evaluate, by audits or other equivalent means, that the provisions of the approved programme are being fully followed. Such evaluations should occur as determined by the Administration, but at least once every five years.

7.4 The interpretation of the provision "the owner of the container shall be responsible for maintaining it in safe condition" (annex I, regulation 2, paragraph 1 of the Convention) should be such that the owner of a container (as defined in article II, paragraph 10 of the Convention) should be held accountable to the Government of any territory on which the container is operated for the safe condition of that container.

7.5 The owner should be bound by the existing safety laws of such a territory and such law or regulation as may implement the control requirements of article VI of the Convention. Nevertheless the methods by which owners achieve, under the provisions of article IV, the safe condition of their containers, that is the appropriate combination of planned maintenance, procedures for refurbishment, refit and repair and the selection of organizations to perform this work, should be their own responsibility. If there is clear evidence for believing that an owner is repeatedly failing to achieve a satisfactory level of safety, the government of the territory in which the owner has his head office of domicile should be requested to ensure that appropriate corrective action is taken.

7.6 The responsibility of the owner to maintain his container in a safe condition includes the responsibility to ensure that any modifications carried out on an approved container do not adversely affect or render inaccurate the information recorded on the Safety Approval Plate. Under the provisions of annex I, chapter V, regulation 11, the owner of a container which has been modified in a manner resulting in structural changes shall notify the Administration or an approved organization duly authorized by it of those changes. The Administration or authorized organization may determine whether the results of the original tests conducted in accordance with annex II for the initial container approval remain valid for the modified container.

7.7 If an owner removes a container from service and it is no longer required to comply with the Convention or does not maintain that container in accordance with the provisions of the Convention, or makes structural modifications without following the procedures in paragraph 7.6 above, the owner must remove the Safety Approval Plate.

8 **Withdrawal of approval** (article IV, paragraph 5)

8.1 With regard to withdrawal of approval, the *Administration concerned* should be considered as the Administration which issued the approval. While any Contracting Party may exercise control over container movement pursuant to article VI, only the Administration which approved the container has the right to withdraw its approval. When approval has been withdrawn, the Administration concerned should require the removal of the Safety Approval Plate.

9 **Acceptance of approvals** (article V)

9.1 Records of approved continuous examination programmes

Administrations should maintain a list of approved continuous examination programmes (ACEP) and make the list publicly available.

10 **Control** (article VI)

10.1 General

10.1.1 This section concerns the control of containers under the Convention and does not address maintenance and examination issues.

10.1.2 For the purposes of effecting control (as envisaged in article VI of the Convention), Contracting Parties should only appoint authorized control officers of government bodies. Article VI requires that such control should be limited to verifying that the container carries a valid Safety Approval Plate, and an ACEP or a valid next examination date (NED) marking, unless there is significant evidence for believing that the condition of the container is such as to create an obvious risk to safety.

10.2 Training of authorized control officers

The Contracting Party exercising control should ensure that authorized control officers have received the necessary training. This training should involve both theoretical and practical instruction.

10.3 Unsafe containers

10.3.1 Control officers who find a container that is in a condition that creates an obvious risk to safety should stop the container until it can be ensured that it is in a safe condition to continue in service.

10.3.2 All containers with serious structural deficiencies in structurally sensitive components (see section 10.4) should be considered to be in a condition that creates an obvious risk to safety.

10.3.3 Control officers should notify the container owner whenever a container is placed under control.

10.3.4 Control officers may permit the onward movement of a container that has been stopped to its ultimate destination providing that it is not lifted from its current means of transport.

10.3.5 Empty containers with serious structural deficiencies to structurally sensitive components are also deemed to place a person in danger. Empty containers are typically repositioned for repair at an owner-selected depot provided they can be safely moved; this can involve either a domestic or an international move. Any damaged container being so repositioned should be handled and transported with due regard to its structural deficiency. Clear signage should be placed on all sides and the top of the damaged container to indicate it is being moved for repairs only.

10.3.6 Empty containers with severe damage that prevents safe lifting of the container, e.g. damaged, misplaced or missing corner fittings or a failure of the connection between side-walls and bottom side rails, should only be moved when carried on a platform-based container, such as a flat rack.

10.3.7 Major damage may be the result of significant impact which could have been caused by improper handling of the container or other containers, or significant movement of the cargo within the container. Therefore, special attention should be given to signs of recent impact damage.

10.3.8 Damage to a container may appear serious without creating an obvious risk to safety. Some damage, such as holes, may infringe customs requirements but may not be structurally significant.

10.4 Structurally sensitive components and definition of serious structural deficiencies for consideration by authorized control officers only

10.4.1 The structurally sensitive components of a container that should be examined for serious deficiencies are the:

.1 top rail;

.2 bottom rail;

.3 header;

.4 sill;

.5 corner posts;

.6 corner and intermediate fittings;

.7 understructure; and

.8 locking rods.

10.4.2 The following criteria should be used by the authorized control officers to make immediate out-of-service determinations or impose transport restrictions. They should not be used as repair and in-service criteria under a CSC ACEP or a periodic examination scheme. Figures 1 to 4 show examples of structurally sensitive components and figure 5 is a flow chart that illustrates the actions to be taken by an authorized control officer.

(i)	(ii)	(iii)	(iv)	(v)	(vi)	(vii)
Structurally sensitive component	**Serious deficiency requiring immediate out-of-service determination**	**Deficiency requiring advice to owner and restrictions for transport**	**Restrictions to be applied in case of deficiencies according to column (iii)**			
			Empty container		**Loaded container**	
			Sea transport	**Other modes**	**Sea transport**	**Other modes**
Top rail	Local deformation to the rail in excess of 60 mm or separation or cracks or tears in the rail material in excess of 45 mm in length (see note 1)	Local deformation to the rail in excess of 40 mm or separation or cracks or tears in the rail material in excess of 10 mm in length (see note 1)	No restrictions	No restrictions	Bottom lifting not allowed; top lifting allowed only by use of spreaders without chains	Bottom lifting not allowed; top lifting allowed only by use of spreaders without chains
	Note 1: On some designs of tank containers the top rail is not a structurally significant component.					
Bottom rail	Local deformation perpendicular to the rail in excess of 100 mm or separation or cracks or tears in the rail material in excess of 75 mm in length (see note 2)	Local deformation perpendicular to the rail in excess of 60 mm or separation or cracks or tears in the rail material: in excess of 25 mm in length in the upper flange; or of web in any length (see note 2)	No restrictions	No restrictions	Lifting at (any) corner fitting not allowed	Lifting at (any) corner fitting not allowed
	Note 2: The rail material does not include the rail's bottom flange.					

(i)	(ii)	(iii)	(iv)	(v)	(vi)	(vii)
Header	Local deformation to the header in excess of 80 mm or cracks or tears in excess of 80 mm in length	Local deformation to the header in excess of 50 mm or cracks or tears in excess of 10 mm in length	Container shall not be overstowed	No restrictions	Container shall not be overstowed	No restrictions
Sill	Local deformation to the sill in excess of 100 mm or cracks or tears in excess of 100 mm in length.	Local deformation to the sill in excess of 60 mm or cracks or tears in excess of 10 mm in length	Container shall not be overstowed	No restrictions	Container shall not be overstowed	No restrictions
Corner posts	Local deformation to the post in excess of 50 mm or cracks or tears in excess of 50 mm in length	Local deformation to the post in excess of 30 mm or cracks or tears of any length	Container shall not be overstowed	No restrictions	Container shall not be overstowed	No restrictions

(i)	(ii)	(iii)	(iv)	(v)	(vi)	(vii)
Corner and intermediate fittings	Missing corner fittings, any through cracks or tears in the fitting, any deformation of the fitting that precludes full engagement of the securing or lifting fittings (see note 3) or any weld separation of adjoining components in excess of 50 mm in length	Weld separation of adjoining components of 50 mm or less	Container shall not be lifted on board a ship if the damaged fittings prevent safe lifting or securing	Container shall be lifted and handled with special care	Container shall not be loaded on board a ship	Container shall be lifted and handled with special care
		Any reduction in the thickness of the plate containing the top aperture that makes it less than 25 mm thick	Container shall be lifted and handled with special care Container shall not be overstowed when twistlocks have to be used	Container shall be lifted and handled with special care	Container shall not be lifted by the top corner fittings	Container shall be lifted and handled with special care
		Any reduction in the thickness of the plate containing the top aperture that makes it less than 26 mm thick	Container shall not be overstowed when fully automatic twistlocks are to be used	Container shall be lifted and handled with special care	Container shall not be used with fully automatic twistlocks	Container shall be lifted and handled with special care
	Note 3: The full engagement of securing or lifting fittings is precluded if there is any deformation of the fitting beyond 5 mm from its original plane, any aperture width greater than 66 mm, any aperture length greater than 127 mm or any reduction in thickness of the plate containing the top aperture that makes it less than 23 mm thick.					

(i)	(ii)	(iii)	(iv)	(v)	(vi)	(vii)
Under-structure	Two or more adjacent cross members missing or detached from the bottom rails; 20% or more of the total number of cross members missing or detached (see note 4)	One or two cross members missing or detached (see note 4)	No restrictions	No restrictions	No restrictions	No restrictions
		More than two cross members missing or detached (see notes 4 and 5)	No restrictions	No restrictions	Maximum payload shall be restricted to 0.5*P*	Maximum payload shall be restricted to 0.5*P*
	Note 4: If onward transport is permitted, it is essential that detached cross members are precluded from falling free. **Note 5:** Careful cargo discharge is required as forklift capability of the understructure might be limited.					
Locking rods	One or more inner locking rods are non-functional (see note 6)	One or more outer locking rods are non-functional (see note 6)	Container shall not be overstowed	No restrictions	Container shall not be overstowed; cargo shall be secured against the container frame and the door shall not be used to absorb acceleration forces; otherwise maximum payload shall be restricted to 0.5*P*	Cargo shall be secured against the container frame and the door shall not be used to absorb acceleration forces; otherwise maximum payload shall be restricted to 0.5*P*
	Note 6: Some containers are designed and approved (and so recorded on the Safety Approval Plate) to operate with one door open or removed.					

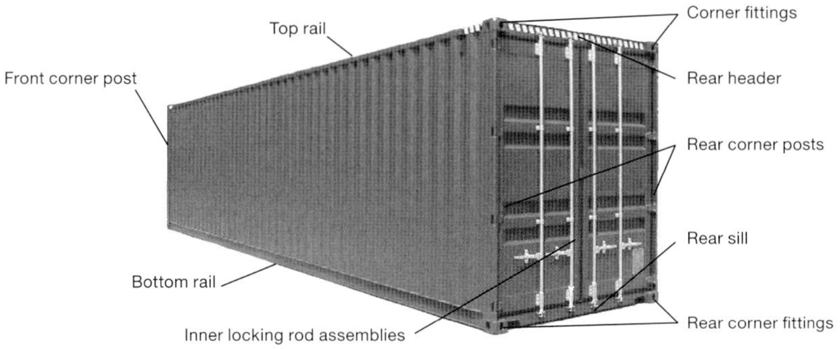

Figure 1

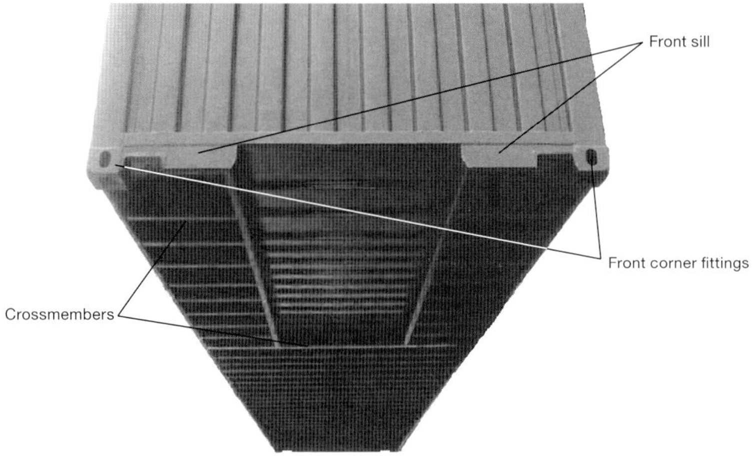

Figure 2

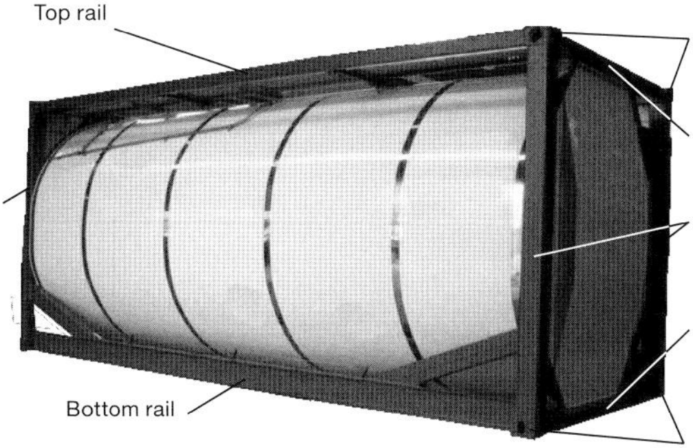

Figure 3

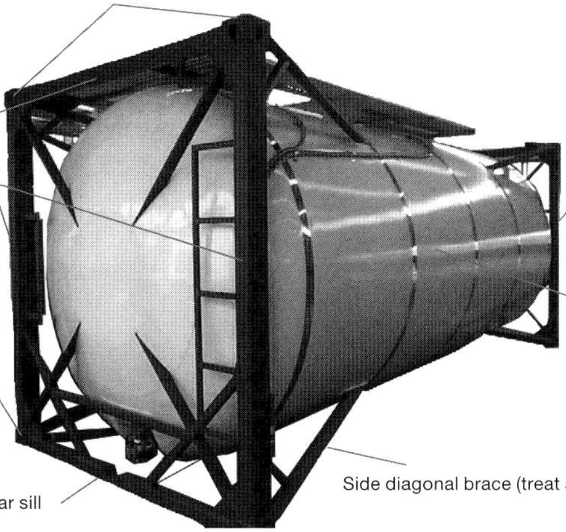

Figure 4

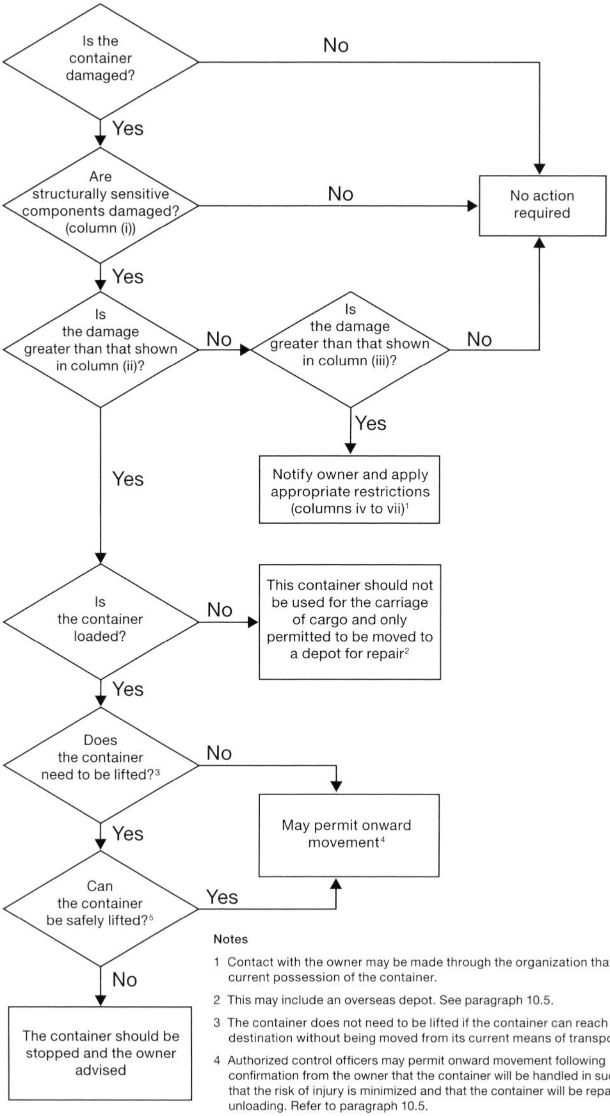

Notes

1 Contact with the owner may be made through the organization that has current possession of the container.

2 This may include an overseas depot. See paragraph 10.5.

3 The container does not need to be lifted if the container can reach its destination without being moved from its current means of transport.

4 Authorized control officers may permit onward movement following confirmation from the owner that the container will be handled in such a way that the risk of injury is minimized and that the container will be repaired after unloading. Refer to paragraph 10.5.

5 The container that has damage to cross members, bottom rails or corner fittings should not be lifted.

Figure 5

10.4.3 The effect of two or more items of damage in the same structurally sensitive component, even though each is less than that specified in the above table, could be equal to, or greater than, the effect of a single item of damage listed in the table. In such circumstances, the control officer may stop the container and seek further guidance from the Contracting Party.

10.4.4 For tank containers, the attachment of the shell to the container frame should also be examined for any readily visible serious structural deficiency comparable to that specified in the table. If any such serious structural deficiency is found in any of these attachments, the control officer should stop the container.

10.4.5 The end frame locking mechanism of platform containers with folding end frames and the hinge pins about which the end frame rotates are structurally sensitive components and should also be inspected for significant damage. Containers with folding end walls that cannot be locked in the erect position should not be moved with the end walls erect.

10.4.6 The deficiencies listed in paragraph 10.4.1 are not exhaustive for all types of containers or all possible deficiencies or combination of deficiencies.

10.5 International movement of containers under control

It is recognized that in any of the cases covered by this section the owner may wish to move a container to another territory where the appropriate corrective action can be more conveniently carried out. Control officers may permit such movements, but should take such measures as may be reasonably practicable to ensure that the movement is carried out safely and that the appropriate corrective action is indeed taken. In particular, the control officer permitting such a movement should consider whether it would be necessary to inform the control officer or officers in the other territory or countries through which the container is to be moved.

10.6 Notification concerning unsafe containers of a given approved series

If a considerable number of containers in a given approved series is found to be unsafe as a result of defects which may have existed prior to approval (article VI, paragraph 2), Administrations should notify the Organization as well as the Contracting Party concerned.

10.7 Containers that are not defective but have no Safety Approval Plate or that have an incorrectly completed plate

Containers that have no Safety Approval Plate or an incorrectly completed Safety Approval Plate should be stopped. However, where evidence can be produced either to the effect that such a container has been approved under the terms of the Convention or to the effect that such a container meets the standards of the Convention, the authority exercising control may permit the container to proceed to its destination for unloading, with the proviso that it shall be plated as expeditiously as may be practicable and not reloaded before it has been correctly plated under the Convention.

10.8 Containers that are "out of date"

A container being maintained under a periodic examination scheme (PES) should be stopped if it is found to have marked on or near to its Safety Approval Plate a next maintenance examination date in the past. However, the competent authority exercising control may permit the container to proceed to its destination for unloading with the proviso that it should be examined and updated as expeditiously as may be practicable and not reloaded before this has been done.

10.9 Containers that are missing their ACEP or NED marking

When there is neither an ACEP nor an NED marking on or near the Safety Approval Plate, the container should be stopped until it can be proven that the container is being operated and maintained under a valid programme. If the container is being operated under an ACEP the container should be allowed to continue its journey and the operator should be notified. The missing marking should be applied after unloading the container at the final destination and prior to its next reloading or at its next interchange, whichever is earlier.

10.10 Containers with defects when approved

Where a container appears to have become unsafe as a result of a defect that may have existed when the design of the container was approved, the Contracting Party that detected the defect should inform the Administration responsible for that approval.

11 Safety Approval Plate (regulation 1)

11.1 The following approaches to complying with certain aspects of the data requirements of the Convention, listed in this section, are deemed to be in conformity therewith.

11.2 A single approval number may be assigned to each owner for all existing containers in a single application for approval which could be entered on line 1 of the plate.

11.3 The example given in line 1 of the model Safety Approval Plate (see appendix to annex I of the Convention) should not be construed to require the inclusion of the date of approval in the approval reference.

11.4 The appendix to annex I of the Convention allows the use of the owner's ISO alphanumeric identification codes or manufacturer's serial numbers on existing containers. Only the manufacturer's serial number should be used as the identification number (line 3) on the Safety Approval Plate for containers approved on or after 14 May 2010. Where the Safety Approval Plate forms part of a larger grouped or consolidated plate (see paragraph 11.9), the manufacturer's serial number may be marked elsewhere on that plate. The owner's ISO alphanumeric identification code may also be shown elsewhere on a consolidated plate.

11.5 Where marking of the end-wall or side-wall strength on the plate is not required (e.g. a container with the end-wall or side-wall strength equal to 0.4*P* or 0.6*P*, respectively), a blank space need not be retained on the Safety Approval Plate for such marking but can be used instead to meet other data requirements of the Convention, e.g. subsequent date marks.

11.6 Where end-wall or side-wall strength is required to be marked on the Safety Approval Plate, this should be done as follows:

in the English language:

END-WALL STRENGTH
SIDE-WALL STRENGTH

in the French language:

RÉSISTANCE DE LA PAROI D'EXTRÉMITÉ
RÉSISTANCE DE LA PAROI LATÉRALE

11.7 In cases where a higher or lower wall strength is to be marked on the Safety Approval Plate, this can be done briefly by referring to the formula related to the payload *P*, e.g. as follows:

SIDE-WALL STRENGTH 0.5*P*

11.8 With respect to the material characteristics of the Safety Approval Plate (see appendix to annex I of the Convention), each Administration, for purposes of approving containers, may define *permanent*, *non-corrosive* and *fireproof* in its own way or simply require that Safety Approval Plates be of a material which it considers meets this definition (e.g. a suitable metal).

11.9 Regulation 1 of annex I requires that the Safety Approval Plate be affixed adjacent to any approval plate issued for official purposes. To comply with this requirement, when practicable, the CSC Safety Approval Plate may be grouped with the data plates required by other international conventions and national requirements on one base plate. The base plate should be conveniently located on the container.

12 Maintenance and examination procedures (regulation 2)

12.1 The Convention allows owners the option of having containers examined at intervals specified in the Convention in accordance with an examination scheme prescribed or approved by the Administration concerned, as set out in regulation 2, paragraph 2, and hereinafter referred to as "periodic examination scheme", or under a continuous examination programme approved by the Administration concerned, as set out in regulation 2, paragraph 3, and hereinafter referred to as "continuous examination programme".*

12.2 Both procedures are intended to ensure that the containers are maintained to the required level of safety and both should be considered equal, provided the Administration is satisfied with the examination scheme used by the owner.

12.3 The owner should be allowed the option of having part of his fleet covered by one examination procedure and the remaining part of his fleet covered by the other procedure, and provision should be made to allow an owner to change the procedure applicable to their containers.

12.4 Elements to be included in the examination

12.4.1 *For containers covered by periodic examination schemes or continuous examination programmes*

12.4.1.1 While Administrations may specify factors to be taken into account in a container examination scheme, it should not be necessary at this time to agree on a specific list of factors or minimum listing of parts of a container which should be included in an examination. However, each examination should include a detailed visual inspection for defects or other safety-related deficiencies or damage which will render the container unsafe and include examination of all structurally significant components of the container, particularly the corner fittings.

* Refer to the Guidelines for development of an approved continuous examination programme (ACEP) (CSC.1/Circ.143).

12.4.1.2 It is accepted that a visual examination of the exterior of the container will normally be sufficient. However, an examination of the interior should also be performed if reasonably practicable (e.g. if the container is empty at the time). Furthermore, the top and underside of the container, including the underside of the lower corner fittings, should be examined. This may be done either with the container supported on a skeletal chassis or, if the examiner considers it necessary, after the container has been lifted onto other supports.

12.4.1.3 The examination of a container should be carried out by a person having such knowledge and experience of containers as will enable him to determine whether it has any defect that could place any person in danger.

12.4.1.4 The person performing the external examination should have the authority to require a more detailed examination of a container if the condition of the container appears to warrant such examination. If there is a possibility of serious structural deficiency in structurally sensitive components (see 10.4 above), measuring tools to fully assess the defects that are noted should be used.

12.4.2 *Additional requirements for containers under a continuous examination programme*

12.4.2.1 Under an approved continuous examination programme a container is subject to examinations and inspections during the course of normal operations. These are:

.1 *thorough examinations,* which are conducted in connection with a major repair, refurbishment, or on-hire/off-hire or depot interchange; and

.2 *routine operating inspections,* which are frequent inspections performed to detect any damage or deterioration that might necessitate corrective action.

12.4.2.2 Thorough examinations should be carried out in accordance with the requirements of the approved examination programme and care should be taken to ensure that any damaged parts or components have been adequately and safely repaired or replaced. Although Administrations may specify factors to be taken into account during routine operating inspections, normally a visual inspection of the exterior and the underside should be sufficient.

12.4.3 *Container markings for examinations*

12.4.3.1 *Containers under a periodic examination scheme – next examination date (NED)*

12.4.3.1.1 The use of decals should be allowed to indicate the date of the first examination and subsequent re-examination of a container examined at intervals specified in the Convention provided that:

.1 the relevant date (month and year) is shown in internationally recognizable words or figures on the decals or on the plate itself;

.2 the date of the first examination for new containers is shown by decals or otherwise on the plate itself as regulation 2.2 of annex I of CSC 1972 requires; and

.3 the decals have a white background with lettering that may be coloured in accordance with the year of next examination as follows:

BROWN	2004	2010	2016
BLUE	2005	2011	2017
YELLOW	2006	2012	2018
RED	2007	2013	etc.
BLACK	2008	2014	
GREEN	2009	2015	

12.4.3.2 *Containers under a continuous examination programme*

12.4.3.2.1 A container examined under an approved continuous examination programme should bear a decal showing the letters ACEP and the identification of the Administration which has granted the approval, in a similar manner to that stated in annex I, appendix 1, paragraph 1. This decal should be placed on or as close as practicable to the Safety Approval Plate.

12.4.4.3 *Containers operated by a lessee*

12.4.4.3.1 Containers marked with an NED but operated by a lessee with an approved continuous examination programme should be re-marked by the fitting of the lessee's ACEP reference decal and removal or covering of the next examination date.

12.4.4.3.2 Containers marked with an ACEP reference but operated by a lessee with a periodic examination scheme (PES) should be re-marked by the removal or covering of the ACEP reference and the fitting of an NED decal following the first examination under the lessee's examination scheme.

12.4.4.4 *For containers built with limited stacking or racking capacity*

Containers tested in accordance with annex II, chapter 2 (Stacking) with an allowable superimposed static stacking weight less than 192,000 kg for their outermost corner posts, or tested in accordance with annex II, chapter 4 (Transverse racking) with forces less than 150 kN, should be conspicuously marked, as required under the relevant ISO standard.*

12.4.5 *Use of decals*

The use of decals for containers under a periodic examination scheme should remain optional and in no way derogate from the relevant provisions of the Convention to which reference is made above. The responsibility for developing and introducing a decal system should remain with the owners.

13 Records of examinations

13.1 The owner should ensure a system is maintained where examination records are kept, which should include the following:

- **.1** the owner's unique serial number of the container;
- **.2** the date on which the examination was carried out;
- **.3** identification of the competent person who carried out the examination;
- **.4** the name and location of the organization where the examination was carried out;
- **.5** the results of the examination; and
- **.6** in the case of a PES, the NED.

13.2 There is no need to standardize the method by which such records should be kept and existing record systems may be accepted. Such records should be auditable and made available within a reasonable time to the Administration on its request. There is no requirement to keep records of routine operating inspections.

* Refer to current standard ISO 6346, Freight containers – Coding, identification and marking.

14 Frequency of examinations

14.1 Containers under a periodic examination scheme

14.1.1 The Convention recognizes that it may be necessary to examine containers more frequently than every 30 months when they are subject to frequent handling and transshipment. It should be borne in mind, however, that any significant reduction in the 30-month interval between examinations would create severe examination control problems. It should be noted that where containers are subjected to frequent handling and transshipment they are also liable to be subjected to frequent checking.

14.1.2 Therefore, in determining whether it is acceptable that the interval between examinations under the Convention should be the maximum of 30 months, proper account should be taken of intermediate examinations, having regard to their extent and to the technical competence of the persons by whom they are performed.

14.2 Containers under a continuous examination programme

14.2.1 Containers examined under an approved continuous examination programme are subject to a thorough examination in connection with a major repair, refurbishment or on-hire/off-hire or depot interchange and in no case less than once every 30 months.

15 Modifications of existing containers

15.1 Applicants for approval of existing containers may be required to certify that, to the best of their knowledge, any modifications previously carried out do not adversely affect safety or the relevance to those containers of the information presented with the application in accordance with annex I, regulation 9, paragraph 1(d)(ii) and (iii). Alternatively, applicants may submit details of the modification for consideration.

15.2 The removal of a door of a container to enable "one door operation" is considered to be a modification that may adversely affect the safety of the container. Consequently it requires specific approval by the Contracting Party and appropriate markings on the Safety Approval Plate, which must remain on the container after the door has been removed.

15.3 Containers that have been subjected to a modification should retain the original date of manufacture on the Safety Approval Plate and add an additional line showing the date when the modification was carried out.

16 Test methods and requirements (annex II)

Containers tested in accordance with the methods described in the relevant ISO standard* should be deemed to have been fully and sufficiently tested for the purposes of the Convention, except that tank containers provided with fork-lift pockets should be additionally tested in accordance with annex II, test 1(B)(i).

17 Stacking test (annex II, chapter 2)

17.1 The following can be used as guidance in interpreting paragraphs 1 and 2 of the stacking test:

> For a 9-high stacking of 24-tonne (24,000 kg/52,915 lb) containers, the mass on the bottom container would be 8 × 24 tonnes (24,000 kg/52,915 lb), i.e. 192 tonnes (192,000 kg/423,320 lb). Thus, in the case of a 24-tonne container with 9-high stacking capability, the plate should indicate: **ALLOWABLE STACKING MASS FOR 1.8*g*: 192,000 kg/423,320 lb**.

17.2 The following may be a useful guidance for determining allowable stacking mass:

> The allowable stacking mass for 1.8*g* may be calculated by assuming a uniform stack loading on the corner post. The stacking test load applied to one corner of the container shall be multiplied by the factor $\frac{4}{1.8}$ and the result expressed in appropriate units.

17.3 The following is a useful example of how the allowable stacking mass could be varied, as prescribed in paragraph 1 of the stacking test:

> If on a particular journey the maximum vertical acceleration on a container can be reliably and effectively limited to 1.2*g*, the allowable stacking mass permitted for that journey would be the allowable stacking mass stamped on the plate multiplied by the ratio of 1.8 to 1.2 (i.e. allowable stacking mass on the plate $\times \frac{1.8}{1.2} =$ stacking mass permitted for the journey).

---

* Refer to current standard ISO 1496, Series 1 Freight containers – Specification and testing.

18 Longitudinal restraint test (Static test) (annex II, chapter 5)

The acceleration of $2g$ should be considered as the usual value for dynamic loads on containers in normal operation when carried by inland modes of transport. The externally applied test forces of $2R$ prescribed for the static test for longitudinal restraint, together with the fulfilment of the criteria of the other prescribed tests, are to ensure that the structural strength of a container is sufficient to withstand the stresses resulting from normal operation.

19 Validity of approvals

Approvals remain valid if the Contracting Party issuing the approval changes, provided the new entity agrees to maintain responsibility for the proper administration of the Convention and the existing approvals. Approvals also remain valid when container ownership changes, provided the new owner continues to maintain the container to a standard and under procedures that are at least as effective as those originally approved.

CSC.1/Circ.143

Guidelines for development of an approved continuous examination programme (ACEP)*

Background

The International Convention for Safe Containers, 1972 (CSC 1972), as amended, requires containers used for international transport, excluding containers specifically designed for air transport, to meet certain safety approval requirements and be periodically examined. Container owners can choose to follow a periodic examination programme (PEP) or may apply to the Administration (Contracting Parties) for approval of a continuous examination programme (ACEP). This document only addresses continuous examination programmes. Therefore, owners desiring to examine containers under a PEP should contact their respective Administration to determine if they have prescribed procedures for periodic examination programmes.

Purpose

The purpose of these Guidelines is to establish a unified approach when developing a continuous examination programme by container owners for submittal to an Administration for approval and when approving continuous examination programmes by Administrations. These Guidelines provide recommendations to help expedite development and approval of examination programmes in accordance with CSC 1972, as amended. Additionally, adherence to these Guidelines will help to establish a means by which details concerning an approved programme can be easily conveyed and communicated by owners to persons responsible for maintaining their containers in accordance with an approved programme.

---

* The Maritime Safety Committee, at its ninety-second session (12 to 21 June 2013), having considered the proposal by the Sub-Committee on Dangerous Goods, Solid Cargoes and Containers, at its seventeenth session, approved the Guidelines for development of an approved continuous examination programme (ACEP) (5 August 2013).

Discussion

Format: In order to provide for ease of evaluation, reference and filing, continuous examination programmes should follow these format recommendations at the time of applications. Programme submittals in hard copy format should be suitably assembled. Alternatively, Administrations may encourage use of electronic media for document submittals. The front cover should clearly identify the container owner. If the submitted programme is completed on behalf of the container owner by another organization, the submitting organization should be referenced on the front cover as well.

1 Covering letter

1.1 Requesting approval for the submitted programme.

2 Company information

2.1 Brief description of company's business operations.

2.2 Brief description of type and quantity of containers to be subject to the programme.

2.3 Company head office contact information. Main phone, fax, email, website and address. Phone number and email of company point-of-contact for ACEP issues, if different from head office.

2.4 Basic organization chart or information detailing the responsibilities of key persons or positions associated with the programme.

2.5 Confirmation that the Company agrees to implement the approved programme and to maintain the safety of containers as prescribed by CSC 1972, as amended.

Note: Owners who operate, manage and maintain their container fleet under a certified quality system should be taken into account by the Authority representative in the evaluation of the documentation.

3 Container marking

3.1 Describe procedures for marking new and existing containers with identification to show that the container is examined under an ACEP as well as the procedure for restoration of damaged or lost ACEP markings.

3.2 Describe the placement of the ACEP label on the container and provide the label image.

3.3 Describe how individual containers are uniquely identified.

3.4 Describe procedures and obligation of the container owner to remove (or not remove) the ACEP label if the container is sold or leased.

4 Container examinations

4.1 Detail which industry-accepted pass/fail criteria are used for container examinations, repair and maintenance. If an owner criterion is used, provide associated methods, scope and criteria for conducting container examinations, repair and maintenance.

4.2 In the case that no industry-accepted pass/fail criteria are used, describe the methods for maintenance criteria that address the design characteristics of the specific containers.

4.3 Describe any procedures for auditing container examinations, either internal or external, by or on behalf of the container owner.

4.4 Detail the maximum time allowed between container examinations. Identify events that trigger a container examination. Describe the procedures to ensure that the maximum time allowed between examinations is not exceeded.

4.5 Describe the methods to ensure that container examinations are conducted by competent persons.

4.6 Describe procedures for repairing and re-examining failed containers.

5 Documentation

5.1 Describe the procedures for recording container examination results and methods for tracking examinations through the use of unique container serial numbers. If contractual personnel or contracted container yards conduct container examinations, detail the process for recording these examinations and the scope of information to be recorded.

5.2 Describe the process for the automated exchange of interchange and/or repair information. In case of non-automated procedures, provide a copy of container owner inspection form(s) or equipment interchange receipt(s) used in the programme.

5.3 Describe the means of identifying containers, their last examination dates and any repair work in their records.

5.4 Describe the procedure to control examination dates and the personnel responsible for control.

5.5 Specify the period of time that records will be retained under the control of the container owner.

5.6 Identify the location where examination records are maintained and the personnel or organization responsible for control of that location.

5.7 Detail examination record availability to the Administration for inspection upon request.

5.8 If applicable, provide details on the inclusion of the programme into the container owner's quality management programme.

5.9 Detail procedures for maintaining a file of training certificates or records for personnel qualified to conduct container examinations and the availability for review by the Administration personnel upon request.

5.10 Describe the procedures for adding, removing and updating containers in the programme.

5.11 Describe the procedure to ensure that only containers equipped with a valid Safety Approval Plate will be included in the programme.

6 Leasing

6.1 Detail how the examination programme of the lessor (owner) company is transferred to the lessee or bailee company and is implemented under lease agreements.

6.2 Provide a sample copy of container lease agreements and identify where the leases are maintained and the personnel and/or organization responsible for control of the location.

7 Container compliance with CSC 1972

7.1 Provide a declaration from the applicant that only containers approved under CSC 1972 are included in the programme.

7.2 Upon request by the Administration, the applicant should provide evidence of approval (e.g. copies of approval certificates or photos of Safety Approval Plates).

8 Conclusion

8.1 Upon results of consideration of the continuous examination programme submitted to the Administration for approval and of the audit to evaluate that all the provisions of ACEP are fulfilled, the Administration should:

- **.1** provide the approval letter; and
- **.2** inform the container owner of their ACEP registration number which includes:
  - **.1** the letters ACEP;
  - **.2** identification of the Contracting Party; and
  - **.3** the assigned number.

8.2 Administrations should make the information on ACEPs publicly available. Such information should include, but may not be limited to:

- **.1** company's name and contact details;
- **.2** identification system of ACEP; and
- **.3** date of ACEP approval.

8.3 Approved continuous examination programmes should be reviewed by the Administration not later than 10 years after approval or reapproval to ensure their continued viability.

8.4 Owners of approved programmes should notify the approving Administration about significant changes as soon as possible. Such changes may include modifications to:

- **.1** contact information;
- **.2** responsibilities;
- **.3** provisions for conducting examinations; and
- **.4** fleet operator.

8.5 Administrations should establish a programme for conducting periodic reviews of approved programmes and periodically enquire about changes made to approved programmes.

Notes

Notes